Celina Maria de Souza Olivindo
Gesinaldo Cândido
Nayara Oliveira

Perceptions and Reflections: Administration and Society

Celina Maria de Souza Olivindo
Gesinaldo Cândido
Nayara Oliveira

Perceptions and Reflections: Administration and Society

for a more reflective society, with collaborative and responsible attitudes

ScienciaScripts

Imprint

Any brand names and product names mentioned in this book are subject to trademark, brand or patent protection and are trademarks or registered trademarks of their respective holders. The use of brand names, product names, common names, trade names, product descriptions etc. even without a particular marking in this work is in no way to be construed to mean that such names may be regarded as unrestricted in respect of trademark and brand protection legislation and could thus be used by anyone.

Cover image: www.ingimage.com

This book is a translation from the original published under ISBN 978-613-9-62877-3.

Publisher:
Sciencia Scripts
is a trademark of
Dodo Books Indian Ocean Ltd. and OmniScriptum S.R.L publishing group

120 High Road, East Finchley, London, N2 9ED, United Kingdom
Str. Armeneasca 28/1, office 1, Chisinau MD-2012, Republic of Moldova, Europe
Printed at: see last page
ISBN: 978-620-7-75303-1

SUMMARY

Perceptions and Reflections: Administration and Society

Celina Maria de Souza Olivindo[1]

Gesinaldo Ataide Càndido[2]

Nayara Cristina da Rocha Oliveira[3]

I.PhD student in Administration - UFPB University Professor, Researcher, Writer and Speaker. PhD student in Administration, Master in Administration from FEAD - MG (2014), Postgraduate in Strategic Management in Human Resources from UFRRJ-RJ (2006), Postgraduate in Methodology of Higher Education from INTA-PI (2008) Graduated in Administration from Faculdade São Francisco de Barreiras-BA (2004). Member of SBEO - Brazilian Society of Organizational Studies, Evaluator of the journal RESEARCH, SOCIETY AND DEVELOPMENT. Member of the Learning and Knowledge Research Group (NAC), UFPB.

2. Full Professor of General Administration at UFCG, Doctorate in Production Engineering from the Federal University of Santa Catarina (2001), Master's Degree in Administration from the Federal University of Paraiba (1995), working on undergraduate courses in Administration and Production Engineering at UFCG. He is a permanent professor in the Postgraduate Programs in Administration at UFPB and UFCG. Head of GEGIT (Group of Studies in Management, Innovation and Technology), registered in the CNPq directory of research groups. Member of the editorial board and evaluator of several scientific journals and referee at several scientific events in Brazil and abroad.

3. Specialist in Strategic People Management - IFPI Graduated in Nursing from the State University of Piaui (2015), Specialization in Gynaecology and Obstetrics and in Strategic People Management, Postgraduate student in Family and Community Health. Researcher in the areas of people management, clinical medicine and alternative treatments (medicinal plants). She has experience in clinical nursing, people management and primary care.

PRESENTATION

To think about life in society is to reflect on habits, customs and shared life. These reflections are a simple summary of various thoughts by authors who are more than recognized in scientific academia, they are recognized in the lives of their readers. Constructing this work was more than a doctoral task, it was a gift that Professor Gesinaldo Ataide allowed me to experience. In my writings, I have tried to reflect on the role of administration in life in society and its new directions, thinking about how to live in this capitalist life that we know, where many have the attitudes of an ostrich. We are living through a post-globalization without knowing ethics and excellence in business very well, so we do need a global debate on the possibilities of a third way, not just for politics, but for global life. Society is at risk, heading towards another modernity with the culture of a new capitalism that makes us think more each day about which path to take, placing us at crossroads of increasingly complex choices, demanding from each one an uncorrupted character that allows ethics to be possible even in a world of such consumerist and immediate consumers. Life today is about limitless consumption, looking to a future with increasingly scarce resources, which is why these reflections are necessary, so that we can all have a prosperous life with sustainable growth and that this life is really good for people and for the planet, which is finite.

Handbook of **Organizational Studies: reflections and new directions.**

The handbook for Organizational Studies brings together reflective thoughts on theories traditionally debated and known in the Organizational Studies environment, as well as discussions in the light of new perspectives from new areas of study. Through intelligent and dense reading, the authors instigate the construction of concepts for us readers outside the comfort zone of the discourses already strongly rooted in the academies of studies on management processes in the world. The texts reflect on the antagonistic process between Critical Theory and Post-Modern Theory, as the popular expression goes "from Oiapoque to Chui", without losing the central focus on the development of organizational theories and practices. Reflecting on this theme is a challenge and a motivation, like believing in something without at least giving yourself the right to doubt its real existence for a moment and thus tread a path that seeks to prove its existence or not.

Reading the *Handbook* takes us into the world of various theoretically controversial uncertainties in the social and historical context of these studies. The theoretical construction described in this handbook revolves around the differences between Critical Theory and Postmodern Approaches to organizational studies. Reading it therefore provokes intellectual and constructive development in the reader. It promotes a break with dogmatic thinking, where certainty is absolute, and takes us into the world of daily construction and constant study in the search for increasingly effective ways of doing management. The author reinforces the need for administrative control to be less and less in the power of labour laws and/or merely behavioural, and for the power of the mind, intellect and thinking to be institutionalized in organizations. However, all this talk has difficulty becoming real. I corroborate the authors' discourse when they warn and strongly point out that there is no point in talking about new theories, that organizations need to be more organic, social and overcome the barrier of Fordism, if the community capable of generating these changes is only willing to empower itself with the theoretical part of the studies, leaving the applicability of these new forms of management only to books, articles and scientific events.

Even though this manual is largely focused on studies of concepts from specific lines of study, there is a clear sense of consistency and veracity in its reports, as well as evidence of the need to evolve studies and practices in the management of organizations, but let's remember, as everything in life always has two sides: reverse and obverse, good and bad, positive and negative, it would be no different for this study. The opposition of some to the reports presented represents the opposition to the certainties described and presented in the manual. The construction of knowledge is thus certain and uncertain, defended and accused at the same time by two sides of the same coin, organizational management, where everyone is trying to discover a single goal and the right way to manage in order to generate more with less.

In the construction of the new, there will always be the roots of others, theories that have already been applied, new and old ideas and ideals. The truth is that the evolution of things, people and the world depends on an interconnected chain between past, present and future. And so the construction of the new takes place and the continuity of life gains new and old reasons to continue.

Thinking about theories reminds us of all the others that lend their essence to give life to so many others. This work contributes to the construction of critical thinking aimed at developing better quality and/or better organized scientific material, awakening the need to produce quality and not more numbers to compose scientific statistics. It provokes a reflection on how to act between the practice of research and the existing social discourse. At this point I would like to point out that, even at the risk of finding many obverses, research in Brazil still means following existing lines, thoughts and methodologies, either that or there is no research. If you want to say what you think, then write it down, publish it and pay for everything, including the consequences of opposing those who think differently. This is construction, growing with differences and not being corrupted by them.

Organizational studies come from a vast sequence of studies in the most varied fields of science, always seeking to break paradigms, building in the midst of metaphors and discourses between Fordism avoiding Marxism developed with positivist methods. The cause and effect relationship described in the Pareto relationship is very representative of the rise of administrative theories; in the quest to take a step forward, there is a need for many more steps back. Understanding the past is an input for new conceptions of science. These dialogues sought to unify and give coherence to management proposals. It is important to emphasize that this manual, like many others, has the central objective of building information so that it can be transformed into knowledge and thus applied in the organizational environment.

Even though at times the authors have placed themselves in a prominent position in science for their research, it is important to say that nothing would be possible today without the foundations of organizational studies in the past. The theories that give rise to the understanding of management are a foundation for the development of so many other works with a strong and consistent basis, so that research is becoming more ethical and correct every day. The relevance of the studies lies not in the result, but above all in the path taken. The authors are aware that their research will be questioned and this is what motivates them to do more every day, but they are careful not to become a Babylonian researcher where everything is smaller than their constructed world and always below their walls and theoretical temple.

So many have passed through the upper echelons of power, of knowledge, of the best sciences when it comes to management. According to history, Weber has been considered the patron, the defender, the one who has the right to speak and write about organizational analysis, and like him, others have been and still are part of this select group of disseminators of their own theories, whether traditional or post-modern. Among the many speeches and analyses contextualized in the reading of this manual, the one that most instigated me to continue reading and drinking from this knowledge is when the author says: "what organizational studies lack today is a shared language and a shared project". The evidence of the need for the centrality of science is defended and I see that it is important, as well as patience and the understanding of knowing how to evaluate what is most important at a given moment, science must be born to collaborate in a shared evolutionary process, yes, but with control and responsibility. You can't just value the parts, forgetting that the whole is the end result that will guarantee true knowledge, for example, that haste doesn't help and that the parts without the whole aren't effective, remember the researcher who killed the oldest tree in the world just to confirm that it was the oldest tree, does that make sense? No, perhaps if we look at it through narcissistic eyes.

Analyzing this manual leads us to think about the management process, as well as raising questions such as: What kind of administration is being built? Is it ideal, possible or just acceptable? Evolving in a world of orthodox people hinders the process of necessary evolution that organizational management is crying out for.

The end of capitalism as we know it.

What is capitalism known as? In plain language, it's an economic and social system whose objective is profit and the accumulation of wealth. It is the most widely adopted system in the world today, which is why the writer Elmar Altvater develops a dialogue on the importance of the evolution of the system, which brings with it negative consequences for society, such as social inequality, concentration of power and money. The end of capitalism as we know it must emerge so that a new one can take its place in society. The analysis in this study provokes and questions what can be done to renew and reinvigorate the outdated financial system. The unbridled desire for money and power generates mass production, thus increasing the supply of products, which in turn causes an increase in the consumption of these products, and so the capitalist network gains space and strength, because in order to meet these offers and demands it is necessary to exploit natural resources in an unbridled way, putting at risk the guarantee of the existence of human beings in a medium space of time.

People forget that money is a character in the middle of the process, it's not for it that we should produce more and more, but for existing needs, but the growing production after the industrial revolution focuses on desires and unconscious consumption, proving a black hole called capitalism that is inconsequential and devastates social, economic and environmental equality. Capitalism as we know it is not concerned with the continuity of processes, it focuses only on the aggregate that money will generate for the coffers of banks, companies and entrepreneurs, forgetting that everything is sustained by the society from which all the inputs for production come, be they natural inputs and/or labor. The author makes use of Max's thinking to understand the relationship between capital and the dominant social system on the world stage. According to Altvanter, it is necessary to intellectually and practically detect possible external shocks and alternatives that mature society, in order to bring about cooperation so that everything happens in a way that favors strengthening the economic system, not as it is, but in a different way that can lead the energetically closed capitalist to balanced dimensions that interact with the environment.

The interesting thing is to realize that everything has a time to happen, one day the capitalism we know was the most suitable financial system for the world, but time passes, processes evolve, people change their preferences and all this causes the changes that are perceived in the world. The reading is not merely an economic analysis, but a reflection on ideologies that involve everyone in the world. Economic growth in the world affects everyone, and above all it affects our certainties about life. For a long time it was believed that the capitalist system was the best way to produce wealth and income, but what can be seen in the light of Altvater is that economic growth, which should solve problems, in capitalism is accompanied by financial crises as well as social and environmental problems. So in the light of these studies, some may say that the end is certain, but there are those who say that anyone who believes in the end of capitalism is a fool - it's utopian, to say the least.

In a world where everything permeates finance, it really is a dream to think of building equality through the capitalist system. In the first few chapters, the analysis circulates around nature and its resources as well as society, talking about alternative energy sources and showing options, advantages and disadvantages. It's intriguing how the author leads the reader through the theme of capitalism, talking about various sources of money that are not positively productive in the system. When the book points out the growth of lubricants through oil extraction, it is a reference to the accelerated process of environmental devastation in the world in favor of savage capitalist development.

In the study of organizations, we see the evolution of markets, the creation of wealth for nations and, above all, that the author's discourse leads us to believe that the capitalist way of production generated wealth and thus reduced economic, social and political problems, facts that do not occur today. How can we talk about the economy and capitalism and not remember interest, taxes and fees? Then capitalism was immersed in sanctions, repressions and financial crises. Fundamental issues such as ethics, morals and values had been lost along the way, and now what existed was a set of numbers that determined what would be done without regard for people or the environment.

The consequences are the worst. Whenever the system collapses, it is the people who pay for it. Raising interest rates is generally the first alternative used to try to adjust to the economic collapse. This increase slows down economic growth because private companies, which are the maintainers of these systems, are the first to be affected by high interest rates. Investments become more expensive, and small and medium-sized companies are prevented from accessing credit, as Altvater says. In order to control the chaos and not allow capitalism alone to take over the system, institutions such as the IMF (International Monetary Fund) and the WTO (World Trade Organization) have intervened by determining single rules for trading on the market. With the intervention of regulatory bodies, the economy has become more solid, and globalization has brought about a more competitive market, thus causing interest rates to fall due to the interference of demand and supply. As with every success, there are also consequences. With the increase in competition, prices fell, but interest rates rose. As a result of high interest rates, investments became more expensive, reducing the demand for money and having a negative impact on economic growth. For Altvater, this situation can be resolved by taking action to bring down interest rates, remembering that for this to happen, companies need to be prepared to live with effective competition from financial markets on a global scale.

The economic system seeks equilibrium, so neither demand can be greater than supply nor the other way around. What the market needs is balance, and this is not achieved by raising or lowering interest rates, but by financial management. It is clear that the author is concerned about building a strong economy, but above all, a sustainable one. The challenge is to generate profits while respecting the limitations of companies, without forgetting to show real concern for the environment, from the simple reduction and conversion of the car fleet to the creation of credible alternatives, as he mentions. And so he asks the world: "Is it possible to have a solidarity economy and with it a solidarity-based treatment of natural resources?

Altvater has faith in the social and/or solidarity economy; he sees in it the possibility of combating the simply capitalist production process. He believes in the principle of equivalence, where money and goods have the same value, in reciprocity regardless of race, ethnicity or gender, encompassing many logics and not just that of exchange, redistribution and this associated with resources, as well as solidarity and justice, because it starts from the collective and not the individual. The end of capitalism as we know it shows an economic and social alternative to a world with ethical, moral and economic principles common to all, where there would be social, environmental and financial profits.

Post-globalization, administration and economic rationality: the ostrich syndrome.

This book makes a different, creative and amusing proposal, while at the same time being serious about what it says. With interesting writing, and at the same time light and firm, the author provokes reflection on the relationship between people and money, brings concepts beyond globalization, talks about post-globalization and management in a way that motivates reading, which continuously takes us to a true immersion in knowledge with each page.

The debate on this topic makes us think about everything from the need to talk about the subject to which paths to take in order to circumvent the real trenches of referees, evaluators and reviewers with a myopic and restricted view of what they alone would be capable of producing. So it's a challenge to publish any subject that goes outside the globally accepted context of academia, publishing houses and research groups. Thinking about publishing must first pass through the sieve of accepting the consequences of the macro exposure of thoughts, particularities. It is therefore interesting and enriching to learn about the theoretical ideology of management in a post-globalization context from a writer who is not silent in the face of breaking paradigms. Dealing with a subject such as how the world economy behaves and how megacorporations act in the face of it is fundamentally important for building a better, more egalitarian society. In a society where the rich get richer every day and the poor get poorer, we are heading towards perpetuating inequality between individuals.

We talk about the future, but we don't prepare it as we want it to be. The author says that the "future we want for our planet can no longer honestly depend on the same categories of thought that presided over the classic formulation of what we call globalization or globalization." In short, how can we generate a different future with the same attitudes as in the past? The unbridled exploitation of natural resources and people can continue with the justification that it is to guarantee a better future. What kind of future can we give to a planet that belongs to everyone with practices of unbridled exploitation of nature and people? Simple, the future of global desertification, be it of natural resources, people or money. Things are happening with a single purpose in business life: money for money's sake, that's the motto. The interesting thing about talking about money is that the author makes it clear that his criticism is not of economic science or economic thinking itself, both of which are correct, but of the actions taken by individuals. The economy in its essence is socialist, it was born to seek a balance between the two sides of the market, supply and demand, but the greed of many multinationals has corrupted the system, centralizing all resources in the hands of the minority and enslaving the majority of workers.

In a society that defends an economic system that is determined purely by supply and demand, it can't be called "economism". Thus, in a system forged with a dialogue of force and representatives of giant classes such as funds and economic organizations, they are unable to prevent the bankruptcy of some economic sectors. The author points out that one possible flaw in the system is the way some economists think: they think exactly and scientifically, using only mathematics to aid their decisions and reflections. As he says, if it were to be like this, there would be no need to educate people in the most diverse areas of knowledge, it would only be necessary to educate them so that they act like real calculators, machines for solving problems. Decisions made on the basis of these devices alone tend to generate unsatisfactory results in the global context of social and economic impacts. Remembering that the economy in its definition should generate social sustainability, it is clear that choices like this are unlikely to do so. The feeling is that nothing can be done about the current economic system.

The purpose of the reading is to get to know the ways in which the vision of the ostrich syndrome intervened in the transformation of the economy, the main thread of the story. The syndrome reflects the behavior of individuals who are unwilling to evolve with the times, choosing to hide in their comfort zones such as position and financial condition rather than contributing to a fairer and more economically viable society for all, thus behaving like ostriches with their heads buried without a vision of the future. It is therefore necessary to understand the distinction between economics and crematistics, the former meaning the conduct of community well-being, while crematistics is the practice of seeking to maximize financial profitability, i.e. the accumulation of wealth. These concepts are found in the past, present and will be in the future. Man was made to live together, in community, so the practice of mathematics means putting the financial perspective above all else. Unfortunately, there is an individualistic and competitive race among people to maximize profit in the short term, thus reinforcing non-social practices. Knowing the possible flaws responsible for failed systems allows us to think of general solutions. It is believed that generations of management students are trained to think according to the system presented, molded, standardized, and are not capable of judging, understanding and analyzing the real and global context of each theory, thus strengthening a tradition of continuity of erroneous attitudes that occurs in the business world.

You can't train individuals who don't recognize the importance of balancing the economic system. There has to be a logic of adequacy between purchasing power and the future buyer, as well as the price accepted for the desired product. The system must produce to satisfy needs and not just desires. The age of things, of uncontrolled consumption, will sink the world under so much garbage. Time has shown the evolution of science, techniques and the entrepreneurial spirit, all just for show, which has only served to legitimize large-scale production and inconsequential consumption. The vision of expansion has deluded everyone who is merely looking to make a profit. The exploitation of humans and nature is what really grew with the capitalist system. Management has evolved and brought with it tools to collaborate with this exploitation, with profit as the primary element for the organization, individualism has predominated and has definitely taken hold. It is necessary to rethink the way we manage: internal ethics, values that preserve the environment and national populations, as well as external ethics and cleaner production methods, would mean better control of negative actions in the world.

The proposal is to update the existence of homo economicus and overcome the practice of individualism in organizations. Managers should be focused on their profits, yes, but those who only look at organizations through this prism will soon be considered inefficient for the job; management should be global, looking at the whole and everyone. The mission is simple to understand and difficult to apply. We can no longer hide behind theories and lines of research defined and aligned in absentia. Empowering is the mission of the world's managers, empowering themselves with the courage to take calculated risks in favor of an evolution in the field of management that benefits everyone. The ideal management is the one that focuses on the whole, worrying about clean production without harming present and future generations as well as the environment, not forgetting the people involved in the process, especially the less favored ones, and in the end generating the profit necessary for the company to do well in the market. Responsibility lies with everyone involved, but the focus is on the way organizations are managed. History shows how much company management can harm people and nature. It's time to promote the real post-globalization revolution and guarantee a better world socially, environmentally and economically for everyone. Let's get our eyes out of the hole and look beyond the existing possibilities, building the new is not easy.

Ethics and excellence: cooperation and integrity in business.

Ethics should be a practice integrated into people, the social and corporate environment, it should be something natural in human relations. Talking about ethics leads us to reflect on habits, processes, progress, as well as the difference between the old and the old, not everything that is old is old and not everything that is old is old. Human deficiency in the practice of ethics is something old, and has dominated relationships for centuries. Talking about ethics, whether in the social field or in the corporate world, means reflecting on the same practices. There is not one ethics for every moment of life, but rather a set of values that determine what it means to be ethical. The importance of this book is based not only on the fact that the author clearly explains ethics and the path it has taken and is taking in society, but also on the fact that he defends ethics as an essential element for strengthening society, people and capitalism. In a world that is becoming more individualistic every day, where those in power are concerned with themselves, where companies are no longer just exploiting resources, but also people and the environment are being seriously devastated, it couldn't be more timely to reflect on the role of ethics in society. So Solomon asks: is it possible to teach ethics?

One of the possible answers is that teaching ethics has become an almost impossible challenge in a world so polluted with more examples and doctrines, another is that teaching ethics is the solution to many challenges, yes, but it is possible. Soon society began to debate and reflect on ethics. The best and largest American newspapers entered the scene and raised the issue, with the *Wall Street Journal, Busines Week and The Economist* advocating the existence of ethical people in the world and especially in the corporate environment. So can ethics be taught? Yes, it can be taught, but not, as many people believe, through training courses or quick training sessions. Ethics "begins with a good education," says Solomon. Ethics teaches us the difference between right and wrong, and it's up to each person to choose what they want to do. As far as companies are concerned, within this philosophy of living ethically, there is still a long way to go before we reach a minimally acceptable level of ethical attitudes. The biggest problem in organizations is not the people who are assumed to be unethical, but the unethical people who are assumed to be ethical.

Milton Friedman says that the social responsibility of business is to increase its profits. I understand and even agree with this statement, but we could reinforce it with Solomon's thought that profits are an essentially important part of an organization that is ethically responsible for everyone. Every day, more and more companies hire young wolves who are hungry to devour everything and everyone in order to become part of the select group of executives in their companies. These young people, in turn, fear losing out or creating an image of incompetence, will go to great lengths to achieve the profits that the organization is aiming for. The problem is not achieving the profits, but the path that they have taken to get to the top. It should be said here that the end is not really justifiable in itself, but that a praiseworthy and correct path is necessary. I believe the author when he says that "only a hard path and perseverance lead to success." The author is questioning an ethics that has become detached from society, seen as part of the whole in itself. Attitudes such as humiliation, harassment, selfishness, dirty play, are increasingly accepted in business as long as they generate profit, so where are the virtues? That's what the author says, they're on fire. We mustn't forget that business is a purely human activity, so it needs virtues, integrity and values. It is not acceptable to turn society into a game board where everything revolves around money and power. Business is above all about social integration and cooperation, not competition. As Solomon says, "it is non-negotiable that business ethics, properly understood, is simply good for business".

The key issue in bad business is the habit of ufanism, jargon, culture and *status* politics. The object of business life has become a game, taking risks and facing challenges is natural, a veritable jungle of save-if-you-can. All for the sake of survival and the cherished social *status, what we* see is the politics of "kill or be killed", and so the days go by and the question arises: how to be ethical in this environment? difficult indeed, but not impossible. Solomon shows us with every reading that an ethical society is possible, but it's not easy. People are individualists, everything revolves around greed. It's historical, it's inherited, we really are the fruit of our environment, but above all we are the result of our choices and attitudes. Let's be motivated by the right motives, not let the myth of the profit motive be the biggest motive used to promote unethical actions in business and in life. Drucker says that the "root of the confusion is the mistaken belief that a person's motivation - the businessman's so-called profit motive - is an explanation of his behavior or his guide to action." Where everything revolves around profit, all motivation is focused solely on the bottom line. Companies use game theory to direct their actions.

It becomes easier to apply due to the understanding that business is clearer, direct and cohesive, while ethics is subjective, imprecise and indeterminate. Therefore, according to him, if ethics were similar to business, it would be possible to make it more effective, and the games of business and life would be fairer, known as fair *play*. The author recalls that this theory was conceived in the middle of the Second World War in a different social context. It was developed with the aim of improving economic and non-human activity, an idea that reinforces corporate attitudes. Games were born from the war environment into the business world, bringing with them the evils of war, encouraging competition and competition. The latter is considered to be the backbone of business, not forgetting that competition is not the motivation for business, but just another obstacle to be overcome within ethical limits, and so another piece of business jargon emerges: *Self-made, an* allusion to the *self*, to individualism, reinforcing the unethical role of professionals. History shows that such self-centeredness has only led to problems in the classes, as even the greatest geniuses of the century had to team up with others in order to prosper and succeed in business.

The idea that one day we will understand companies and businesses is the motivation for our daily persistence to get it right. Corporate life is life, and as such must be understood with a set of ethical and moral values. Everything is produced for people with the sole aim of making a profit rather than understanding people's needs and desires. It is therefore essential to serve people with respect for society, nature and business. It's an interconnected network, everything is connected, the old and the old, tradition and modernity, but it can't be treated as an irrelevance that nothing is possible without respect for the basic principles of ethics. Education is the basis, the beginning, the means and the end of the shared process that ethics requires of human values in a society devoid of them. We can't let selfishness, envy and resentment defeat our virtues and charisma. We can collaborate to build better people in every sense, by going through moral labyrinths, or rather, by making our choices with moral courage, as Solomon puts it. This courage is the divider when it comes to the ethical evolution of the individual in the professional, personal and social spheres. We can contribute by example and with a dedication to teaching by learning.

The global debate on the third way.

The debate on the third way is a reflection on a new path to be taken in an attempt to find a new way of looking at the same thing or situation. A solution to something that is no longer working with the existing options, and a new way of looking at human relations in the world. Originating from the clash between public policies and society, the third way is born as a choice, an option, for those who no longer recognize themselves in existing thinking. The discourse on the third way has progressed, but since the launch of this book in 2007, the speed apparently set is a slow march. It is clear that this way of looking at the classes and the world is a possible option for building a fairer and more equal society. Seen as a modernizing social democracy, or rather, a modernizing left, according to Giddens, the Third Way strengthens its essence within Max's ideology, a theoretical current that has been strongly established since its emergence. Marxism shows society specific methods for a more social analysis of factors in society that are considered modern, especially those linked to class conflicts and the productive organization of which paths would be the most appropriate and fair for everyone.

The spread of third way thinking is fostering change in the world, as is the rise of individualism. Throughout history, there have been two sides to the political clashes: those who want a society of solidarity and inclusion, where everyone can be part of history, and those who deny every desire for inclusion and solidarity, the so-called right-wingers, or rather the second way. The world needs a balance not only socially, politically, economically and/or environmentally, but globally, everything must be in balance. This is why the ideology of the third way tends to have so much influence on the global market. It has the activist role for governments of restoring, renewing and oxygenating public and why not private institutions with new air.

So what does this ideology or term mean? The third way generally refers to the idea of a conciliator, a moderator between two existing extreme paths, a link or even a middle ground between two opposing visions. Those who follow the ideological current of the third way argue that the philosophy of "take from the rich and give to the poor" should continue to guide action, but in a rational and coherent way. This should be done through inclusive social policies as well as fair economic plans, where those who have more should pay in proportion and vice versa. Ideology is a utopia for many. For example, the Third Way would like to combine the advantages of capitalism and the advantages of socialism in the same context. Citizenship must therefore be applied to everyone with the aim of creating an egalitarian society. Rulers, civil society, social organizations and class entities must join the current of the third way in order to promote a dynamic economy, the promotion of full employment, the intensification of social and economic policies in harmony, a welfare state, thus reducing inequalities and crime, all forged with public policies that are adept at managing crises in all areas, including the environment. Giddens says that "third way politics

has a lot of power, since parties or governments in all parts of the world need to respond to the fact that the other two ways no longer apply". I honestly believe that whether it's the first, second and/or third way, they won't work if society isn't willing to take on its role in this ideology, nothing will be different from the times of the slaves, the change is that today rules are broken to enslave and not before.

To better understand the emergence of the third way, we need to go back to 1950/60 and remember Keynesian theory and how it interacted with the environment, when it defended the idea of government intervention in the economy in order to guarantee small jobs, as well as understanding the growth of neoliberalism ten years later, In the 1970s and 80s, the other side of the Keynesian coin, the neoliberals, studied and encouraged the principles of classical liberalism in the light of the need for a regulatory and welfare state that should have control of the system and the market. It was precisely from this divergence of opinion between the two sides of the same coin that the so-called third way was born in the 90s. It was born with the aim of being the solution to this clash between socialism and liberalism. However, this is not exactly what we saw with its birth. The then dreamed of and idealized third way, comes much more as a philosophy and a wealth of theorists, politicians, entrepreneurs and civilians all seeking to be heard than to act to implement the global thinking of the third option. In particular, I am a supporter of third way thinking and ideology, as it is more consistent with my values and knowledge of the world. I agree with what he says: "The collective interest can only be built on the basis of the things we share." The current is cohesive in its lines of thought and consolidates itself through speeches such as: the third way considers politics to be an exercise in persuasion and the transmission of values, it fights for people's moral values, remembering that it must follow a different set of priorities, such as education, entrepreneurship and rewards for effort, but all on the perception that things are to be Shared and not Individualized. The struggle used to be about the simple concept of capital and work, but it has changed to a concept of values and society.

Social welfare is no longer seen as something distant from reality, it is essential for the maintenance of the state. Investment in financial capital is no longer enough; social investment is necessary. Balance in the market comes from these two investments, capital and social. The recipe is simple: implement social programs that generate income that can be returned to the market through negotiations between supply and demand and thus move the financial network and contribute positively to economic growth. The best thing is that social development goes beyond that, it encourages the formation of human capital, the accumulation of assets and the mobilization of social capital. Talking about equality is so invigorating and motivating, but as soon as we see the extent of the progress that has been made with so much noise, we realize that the road is long and that there are many struggles to be fought before we reach the long-awaited third way for humanity. Strengthening the educational base and ethics are viable solutions for the growth of the current. Equality and inequality don't only lie in one's financial capacity, but in the way we treat each other. Ethical, committed and responsible governments are the solution.

We believe in harmony between powers, governments and society. There are some obstacles that must be overcome to guarantee this harmony. Governments should not choose a path but should be the very path of conduct and prosperity for society as a whole, companies should not corrupt themselves and should play their role ethically and effectively, interacting with the capitalist and socialist community without ties but subordinated to their freedom and solidarity. The practice of truth is liberating in all spheres of the world. Democracy must be fully exercised, it must not be seen as a commodity to be negotiated, but as the result of a people living together, the freedom of choice must be respected. The author talks about using the third way as a method, a means, a bridge, a link, a strategy for doing business responsibly and ethically; if we were the people we deserve to be, we would be the third way even before the idea was born. It is clear that the current explained here must be applied and replicated within a critical and modern context. Business must be ethical, not the minority as we see it. There are already companies that have adopted the ideology of the third way in their ventures, and I congratulate them. In reality, we need growth with knowledge, expansion with more human demands, less consumption, more nature. We need to integrate the world in an ethical and moral movement, socialism is necessary, so is capitalism, and the third way is an option to promote integration. Well-being must be sustainably integrated into society, capitalism and nature, then there will be a balance.

Risk society: towards another modernity.

A study of the evolution and application of the word "post" in a capitalist, socialist, entrepreneurial and global scenario. The author discusses the impact of this word in the midst of events that took place in past centuries, and leads us to reflect on the impact of post-modernity in the face of the existence of "post" for everything. A word conceptualized by the author as the particle "post" or, advance, late, ultra, it plays an important role in understanding the future that was already announced in the present, according to Beck. Understanding this concept is essential to understanding social development within an industrial society that is increasingly traditional and modern at the same time. There is a fine line that explains the difference between the modernization of tradition and the modernization of industrial society.

As the author says, one originates in the traditional form, or existence itself takes care of it, and the other is more complex through reflection, but it takes a long time and is delicate to achieve. In a dialogue that seems at times to be against modernity and then says that it is necessary, the author draws more attention to the fact that society is being immersed in so many old novelties. What can be understood is that in the midst of so many paraphrased phrases, the central aim of the work is to reflect on historical thoughts in the social field in paradox to industrial society, which the author breaks down into two ways, the first approach referring to the production of wealth and then the perception of the production of risk. One is dominated by the logic of production and the other goes in the opposite direction, where the production of risk is increasingly dominant in the business environment. Living without risk has never been an option, but rather a question of management, in which case it fits very well with administration. I believe that the author will provoke reflection by making analogies with historical events, not just because they were catastrophes, but because they involved several nations.

It's a debate between producing without sharing or sharing what doesn't exist. The industrial production that brought mass wealth was not associated with social thinking, so the eminent risk that has always existed and that exists every day is that fewer become rich and many become poor, is the risk of promoting production, especially modernized production, where technology provides services for many and increases unemployment in some areas of the market. This idea is reinforced when Beck Urich says that "modernization means the technological leap of rationalization and the transformation of work and organization, encompassing much more besides: changes in social characters and lifestyles, power structures, politics and our beliefs." It's not just a question of human submission to economic goods, but it goes beyond that: we have to look above all at the problems arising from economic development itself. It's not a question of stopping production, but of looking beyond capital, as he himself says, the risks of industrial development are as old as he himself, the question is to integrate the two sides of the same coin, tradition and modernity, economic and social. It's motivating and saddening to recognize that the author's thoughts are eternalized in these pages written decades ago. It's motivating to know that the fight for social and productive balance has been going on for years, but saddening when you realize that today it's just as flawed as before in this regard, to recognize that since 1986 a fight has been going on that should have already been successful, and what we have as a result is cynicism in the statistics that continue to mask the truth of the numbers. As early as 1986, Urich said that the deficit in social thinking was growing by the day. Thus the reinforcement that the expression 'being at risk' denotes living in an environment composed of mistrust, where at any moment a disaster can arise without prediction or announcement, reinforces the certainty that risk is present at every moment of human existence.

It's important to emphasize that the author isn't defending side A or B, but rather the idea that one can't exist without the other. If the rationality of science or social science is lacking, it's as if there's just a void. Decisions must be made taking both forms of reasoning into account, or there's a great risk of being blind to the situation. The world has always been global, but only with connectivity have we come to talk about globalization. Taking the boomerang concept as a basis for this statement, we can see that globalization is contained within it. This effect is society's response to the choices made by its participants, which can reflect threats directly to human life, the environment, the economy in a direct or indirect way, ethics must be part of this process of choices, the risk society is lived in society and not individually, according to Urich risks are a "bottomless barrii of needs" that cannot be closed, in turn these needs originate from people. The possible consequences of individualistic acts and endless needs is a mismatch in the relationship between nature and society. Society and its subsystems, such as the economy, politics, family and culture, need to understand that they are not autonomous from nature, that they can live without it. As Urich says in other words, "nature has become politicized because the extent to which nature circulates is used within the system, even in the hands of scientists." There are many dimensions to society, but the individualization of social inequality is one of the most ferocious, born out of the process of free wage labour in modern capitalism, the democratic conditions of the masses, bringing with it mass unemployment and professional disqualification.

However, it's not a question of forgetting everything, of putting things off until later. Individualism fosters class evolution, mixing people up in social cycles measured by money, and thus classifying people by those places they can go and those they can't. In theoretical terms, Urich takes us through what happened in Russia, Germany and the industrialized Western states towards that modern society he so desires. In theoretical terms, Urich shows us what has happened in Russia, Germany and the industrialized Western states in terms of the industrialization of work towards the modern society he so desires. He shows us how the elevator effect still exists today and interferes in people's social lives. Lifespan, working hours and salaried income are three components that have changed life in society. From a relationship perspective, this effect has generated even more inequality in the relationship between work and life. One of the aspects of these inequalities is the fact that in parallel with paid work, the reduction in working hours with the advent of labor rules, men and women began to have more time for the family environment, and the fact that men are idle in domestic activities and women are not, brought more discussion to the subject. The fact that women fought for the right to their own money took them away from the concept of "domestic furniture", as the author puts it, and made them providers of resources, requiring them to be more educated, more mobile, more aware of their own interests, and as a result of this evolution, it brought the social individualism that had affected society into the home.

Reading this book gives us a clear objective: we cannot accept the myth of the unpredictability of the effects of what has been done, it's like saying that we don't know what will grow if we plant a watermelon seed. It's easy to blame the system, be it political, economic or social. The feeling is one of revolt and discontent and a great helplessness in the face of everything we become aware of and do nothing about. To drink in this knowledge and produce nothing in favor of a healthy and prosperous debate is desperate. So the dissemination of this work, whether in the classroom, in a conversation or in articles, is an option for us to collaborate in the construction of a modern and ethical society that is responsible towards people and the environment.

The culture of the new capitalism.

The interesting thing about studying capitalism is that everything circulates around three basic points. The first is the human being, and it's logical, because everything in the world happens for him and to him, as the 1962 Port Huron declaration says. The second point is what gives life to capitalism, money, currency, and the third point is the quest for power, not power granted, but power won by means not so celebrated as oppression and/or tyranny, but power that comes from the desire of others to follow you, I believe the most coveted. The statement reads: "We will replace power based on possession, privilege or economic status with power and uniqueness based on love, reflection, reason and creativity." Management processes follow the bureaucratic trend of administering, through flows, power and the exploitation of labor. Capitalism gives the meaning to everything and the reasons for all choices. Everything revolves around increasing individual wealth in an increasingly capitalist society.

Growing economic inequalities, social and political instability are key factors in community life, but they shouldn't necessarily exist in large proportions. This is why the debate on a new capitalist culture, standards, habits, values and morals must be restructured and strengthened. What values and practices are capable of keeping people together in such a demotivating, difficult-to-live-with scenario? A culture is created not by one person, but by an entire community. The author says that the problem of keeping a culture alive is not limited to a question of its scope, but rather the profile of the human being who is capable of thriving in the unstable social conditions that are increasingly common in society. He points out three characteristics that each individual must have in order to thrive in this new competitive culture. The first relates to respect for time, taking care of interpersonal relationships and ourselves, especially at a time when institutions no longer guarantee continuity of work for anyone. The second relates to talent, which is something individual. We must develop new skills and discover abilities and competencies, and remember that talent is not a question of culture but must be seen as an action focused on meritocracy, doing what is deserved. The third characteristic has to do with the power to let go, to let go of what belongs to you, which means that everything I did up until yesterday doesn't guarantee that I'll have a job tomorrow. Following these three suggestions, we would have the ideal man or woman.

This study is the result of a sequence of theoretical and documentary studies and interviews with workers and managers closest to the global center. The work shows the changes that have been taking place in relations between work and society. One of the feelings found in the author's studies is the individual's fear of becoming obsolete, disposable, replaced by technology and even becoming old in the light of learning. What motivates the debate on this topic is the quest to understand this relationship between the new capitalism and what already exists. Three themes underpin this conversation: work, talent and consumption, all three of which have one thing in common: the human being, the central key to the universe. The modern economy is full of instability in global production, in the productive markets and in the finances resulting from these new technologies. This instability has given rise to the need for creative people and companies. At the beginning of the 19th century, routine was associated with job instability, and not only the workers but also the companies themselves lacked strength and protection. In search of this protection, companies began to test ways of managing. One of the models applied to companies was the military model in Germany. This model showed its efficiency from Bismarck's point of view, in the name of peace and the prevention of revolution, that the poorer the worker, the better established he was in the company, the less willing he would be to revolt against the company, unlike the employee who lived in an opposite situation, At this stage, the foundation of politics was social capitalism, and ironically, as this militarized form of social capitalism spread, business made a profit, because investors were looking for more predictable results.

The perception is that bureaucracy becomes the ideal and more perfected model for capitalism than the market. That's when the author says that "Time is at the heart of militarized social capitalism: a long-term, cumulative and, above all, predictable time" affecting companies and people. This debate is further reinforced by the thesis that the militarization of the system is based on the institutionalization of a culture that revolves around *Bildung,* i.e. that which by "formation" or "culture" carries with it the meaning of a harmonious formation of the whole personality. And through the intervention of the *Bildung,* generations of different cultures are created, but strengthened within their own worlds, such as those who live in Silicon Valley, the so-called technocrats who live a totally different logic from that of the bureaucrats. Two visions of the same social capitalist system, Sennett puts very well the relationship between fear and the desire to move on to new concepts, to understand the cultural difference between the new and the old, to allowâ

a deeper understanding of the life of the institutions. Militarism effectively offers immediate gratification in the service of practice and solidarity with comrades in uniform; this is the idealized feeling for organizations. Towards the end of the 20th century, three important changes in organizations tended to shift the solid pillars of militarized social capitalism. The first change was the shift from managerial power to shareholder power, the second change was the preference for short-term results, and the third change, called the "iron cage", was the development of new technologies and mass communication. So it's clear that inequality has become the achilles heel of the modern economy. Bureaucracies plunged into a trance of reorganization and elimination of intermediate layers could lose the layer of communication, the driving force behind the balance between classes.

What is highlighted in this study is the relationship between old and new, centered on the study of capitalism and the agents involved in the context, from personal capital to the relationship between power and money, linked to the social. Naturally, in a scenario of instability, fear is present, and understanding oneself is a good start in order to have a vision of where one is and where one is going. In fact, the relationship between people and companies has improved over time, trying to understand the basic issues that still persist, such as functional instability, the lack of skills and competences on the part of some. The market lacks talent, professionals who have expertise in what they do, knowledge and power. We live in a consumerist policy, and we need to be prepared for this reality. The interference of sciences such as administration, marketing, socialism and others requires human beings to have the intellectual capacity to promote development. The very idea of democracy requires everyone to have prior knowledge of things so that there can be fair and balanced mediation and discussion between the parties. What the author shows us is that nothing is perfect and everything must be mediated. According to him, bureaucracy can unite as well as oppress; the difference lies in the dose applied. Life in society must be a balance between desires and wants, power and concession, poor and rich, large and small. Efforts must be made to shape institutions that are committed to providing workers with the continuity and sustainability that organizations need, as well as sharing jobs; we must be useful, provide status and live with fullness and commitment to society.

Capitalism at the crossroads.

The crossroads in the progress of life in society comes from responding to the clamor of desires that exceed your needs. The crossroads at which more and more individualistic people decide the future of a nation. Hart's work is an enjoyable read about the real reason why the world is living at a crossroads in their lives. Organizational decisions are affecting the world as a whole on large scales, and management can no longer be done thinking only of local impacts, but above all of the global universe. At a time when man has even sent a car into space with the aim of parking it on the moon, we should no longer think about local or even national issues, but about the universe: what are the consequences of my choices for the environment, society and the universe? Hart makes the following acceptable mission statement. "Short-term profits cannot result in long-term sustainability", in other words, lasting results don't come from hasty, unplanned decisions. Sustainable companies are not born overnight, they need to be planted and nurtured. This is how a society is born that is committed to social and environmental issues, and not just to profit. Not that profit is bad, but profit with responsibility lasts longer. And as Dr. Fisk Johnson, chairman of the Johnson and Johnson companies, says, "there is honor and value in companies". I believe this too, and that's why I've chosen to study ways to corroborate and strengthen thoughts like those of Hart and Johnson.

His work makes us think about how the world has shrunk in space for every living individual, and that the natural resources that once served 2 billion will now serve 8 billion, and we still have to face irregular deforestation, water pollution and the extinction of species that are essential for harmonious life on the planet. We really are at a crossroads, choosing today is fundamental, but making the right choice is a matter of life and death. There is a worrying panorama, but it brings with it opportunities to change some of our corporate actions and community life. What we see are countries that claim to hold power in endless civil wars, others overpopulated with no more space for their people, and even those that degrade their own reserves, and all this in the name of what? A revolution without measure and without logical purpose, that's how I read between the lines of this work. Everyone is looking for a place in the shade, where they can be happy, have their needs met and live in harmony with each other, so if we have all this by doing less and respecting people and nature, what makes me always want more things that wouldn't even serve me? The hunger for power is quite obvious, and that leads us to succumb. Corporations have already realized that not recognizing the importance of sustainable management has important implications. Everything has two sides, and it's no different with companies. There are two sides, one of which is led by the voices of the globalized economy with its very dark side.

At this crossroads, global capitalism is facing yet another moment of choice. Companies need to evolve, change their attitudes, or the road will be more difficult. Some say that capitalism as we know it is on a downward path. Hart says that "sustainable global enterprise thus represents the potential for a new attitude in the private sector" and I wholeheartedly agree. For a long time, managers used to say the famous phrase "take, use and dispose", which is harder to find in capitalism. As companies produced more, they polluted just as much. This reality generated a growing unease in the system, and in the 1980s the green revolution emerged, trying to motivate companies to pollute and degrade less, through a policy of market-based incentives and permits. This change proved to be effective, and developed through innovation and quality management. This was evidenced in the 1980s when Japanese companies gained market share from their US competitors with low-cost quality products. And as the green revolution grew, companies and leaders began to turn their energy and attention more towards proactive strategies to reduce the waste of resources or their reuse, actions that will predominate until 2018. Clean production has always been and still is the most appropriate option.

Other initiatives have emerged with the green revolution, and have overturned the myth that having sustainable attitudes is expensive for companies; on the contrary, they are opportunities for companies to develop and improve their performance. It is worth pointing out that any revolution, especially when it comes to economic resources, cannot be achieved on its own. Strategies must be put together and forces must be joined. As the author shows, a revolution takes time to generate change and the green revolution was no different. The good thing is that the seeds of sustainability and the use of clean technologies have been planted by the business community, the result of a struggle. It is important to get to know the environment so that we can act within a situation and only then establish the bases to be followed. Whenever we hear about capitalism, it always brings us to a crossroads of choices and which one is the best. The collision of the worlds of sustainability and economics is a strong clash that runs counter to each other, and I look forward to the day when both sides indicate that they are heading in the same direction.

As Hart says, the challenge is to "develop a sustainable global economy", an economy that the planet can support - that's a strong expression, it makes me afraid of what to expect in the future. For there to be sustainability, the stabilization that the author talks about is necessary, as well as the reduction of the impacts caused by man on the environment.

What is noticeable when reading Hart's work is the need for corporations to reinvent themselves on sustainable issues. All the case studies presented throughout the book show sustainable actions that can be copied and adapted to different realities around the world, taking into account current political and economic legislation. Organizations do need to reinvent themselves, both in the way they manage staff and in their cost structures, and I would venture to say that one area is linked to the other. Organizations need to align themselves with the times in which the world is living, establish their missions, visions, values and businesses, taking into account every particularity of the moment and not forgetting that they must not be static but flexible to change. It is therefore of the utmost importance that organizations open up the necessary spaces for new innovative ventures based on unique technologies and markets at the base of the pyramid to flourish. All this only means is that these ventures will make money, because on the contrary, as the author says, there's no reason why there shouldn't be profits right from the start.

In order for everything to run smoothly, organizational processes need to be aligned. In addition to the organizational structure and formal systems, informal processes, known as cultural processes, need to be aligned within companies. The author believes that these processes could be the key to resolving this crossroads we are at. The hardest part is bringing about a change in the way people behave, but once the processes are changed, this barrier disappears and people tend to follow the model. As has already been seen in the market with the use of programs such as Six Sigma, Reengineering, Total Quality and others. The freedom for companies to act and create their own production strategy is a predominant factor in corporate growth, so the generation of processes that focus on the creation of sustainable technologies and companies is a tool that is little used in large corporations, perhaps because of the lack of freedom to be creative and innovative.

The corrosion of character: personal consequences of work in the new capitalism.

The title of the work makes us think and want to read the discourse to be found inside the book. On the way to getting to know the book and the thoughts expressed in it, some words recur, both in reading and in research on the subject, words such as Accessibility, time, work, cost, progress, capitalism and corrosion of character, words that along the way instigate the reader's curiosity to drink this water and thus be able to better understand the relationship between man and man as well as man and capital as well as everything around the old and new worlds. To understand the corrosion of character is to understand each part of this whole, first of all corrosion, which can be understood as the gradual wear and tear of character in people's lives, or even as the destruction of rocks, metal, rivers and so on, what matters means only one thing: wear and tear, the disappearance of something, and this almost made me fall off my chair, because putting two words with such strong meanings together in the same sentence causes a certain fear for the future of humanity. If corrosion is disposal, and character is a set of characteristics and traits specific to a human being, the author is saying between the lines that people are losing what determines who they are.

To understand this better, Sennet explains it in a flow of thoughts that begins, as he says, adrift, alluding to capitalism that tries to overcome character, followed by the figure of routine, which doesn't let us get out of our routine, no matter how bad it is, but all is not lost, but the visit of Aexibility arrives to allow time to be restructured, The important thing is for humanity to know that with a strong character, ethics aligned with society, the remedy for failure is the community itself. In pursuit of the dream of having money and power, family values have been lost along the way. Every day, children exchange everything they have been taught for promising opportunities, no matter what the price, how many times they have to move company or city, how many people they have left behind, the dream is to keep trying to dodge time to earn more money and not have time to spend on what really matters, This statement is contextualized by Sennet when he describes that "the classic American residential area was a bedroom community", communities no longer strengthen relationships with their surroundings, nor do they even know them, here I understood the meaning of the corrosion of character, values and detachment from people and attachment to things, but the light at the end of the tunnel appears, and there are those who believe that example is the natural way, and not simply telling children to do what you want. So the watershed of character and quality of work has been identified.

The author affirms and I support what he says, the quality of a job is not associated with a person's character, they are two paths that need to be taken for success, but they must be taken at the same time on different lines. People's exaggerated hunger for daily changes in their lives is generating this corrosion in their character. James Champy says that the "market can be driven by the consumer as never before in history" - in fact, it already is, we live in the era of pure, mindless consumerism. Instability makes organizations need to be more flexible and reduce bureaucracy. Today's management systems in large companies are flatter, less hierarchical and much more flexible. The bonds established must be strong, the problem is the consequences between people and work and that the erosion of character is weakening the family, cooperative objectives must exist to maintain individual objectives and vice versa. This relationship shouldn't only look at the short term; the issue is that companies focus on the short term and in families the relationship is long-lasting. However, as Sennet says, "modern society is in revolt against routine, bureaucratic time, which can paralyze work, government and other institutions". Routine has not been seen as a bad thing, it has even helped capitalism, it is portrayed in books, but we understand that everything has two sides, and the one that wins is the one you believe to be ideal. I like Adam Smith's phrase that says "routine coarsens the spirit" even if we add the dark side of capitalism, the new world and its ramifications with consumerism, capitalism, the rush for everything pushes us out of our moral, normal and routine boundaries, we are ready to adapt to the new and the old, the rich and the poor, time and work is not an option but a consequence.

Character seems to be formed by history and its unpredictable twists and turns, so once you've molded a routine you don't have long to wait. An unknown author once said that if you want a different result, do things differently, don't get used to what you have until death comes. There is a dividing line on the question of routine, the new language of flexibility suggests that routine is dying in the dynamic sectors of the economy, while most of the workforce remains ensconced in the circle of Fordism. I believe that flexibility is here to stay because those repetitive and routine jobs, if not adapted to each human being seen as unique, will not prosper. The author asks how flexibility can make human beings more engaged. In my opinion, the answer is simple, but not easy. Looking at the other person as a whole, respecting their limits, character and values, is a good way to achieve this. People only commit themselves to what they recognize or what they see as the future of what they do. Sennett says that "ideally, flexible human behavior should have the same strength, be adaptable to changing circumstances, but not broken by them". However, we must remember that there must be limits to how far people will have to bend, or we will leave a socialist, democratic society and move on to a new model of enslavement.

We are immersed in the need to seek legitimacy, be it social, financial, power, fame, professional or family. Society is afraid of being someone unreadable, "what matters is how much people stand out from the masses" how many *Clicks and Likes they* have received, the quest to answer the question am I good enough? And that's the answer to flexibility. As for routine, the answer is: at what? Regardless of the answer, the risks of not accepting the answers are real. Choices have always led people down uncertain paths, so it's best to choose in a way that minimizes these uncertainties. I believe that a good advisor for making the best choices is fear, not fear that prevents you from doing something, but fear that gives you good, cohesive reasons why you should or shouldn't do it. And in line with this fear, an overdose of ethics will do just fine. So Sennett puts it this way, "the superficialities of modern society are more degrading than the surfaces and masks of art". Look around you, if you look different from where you live, it's because you need to recognize yourself, know where you're going and whether you're in the right place. People miss real human relationships that have lasting goals, and not just for a season because that has an end. Recognizing where we are and where we want to go doesn't prevent failure, but it does give us ways to grow and, if necessary, to start again as many times as necessary. Don't limit yourself to famous motivational phrases, don't buy a book with a ready-made recipe, the important thing is that you know where you want to go, set the controls for yourself, don't forget that people are important in this process, have character and be ethical, and you'll soon be achieving every goal you set, not in motherhood, but in your intelligence capable of discerning right from wrong.

When business isn't just business.

Business isn't just business when everyone involved in the business cycle wins. One of the most intelligent ways of doing business can be said to be win-win. On the one hand, traders eager to make a profit, on the other, individuals with increasingly latent desires, it's a dance where both sides want to dance, but there is a mismatch, there are still those who haven't understood the correct melody of the dance and step on their partner's toes in the dance. That's when you can say that business is just business, there's always the other person's interpretation, their particular understanding of something or someone, as well as the values and feelings involved in business. To start reflecting on the context of Ruggie's work is to remember at this point that the world has correct, ethical and humane options for living. In the midst of so many readings, I felt so small in my world, and I realized how much I have to learn and add to my city, state and, perhaps, country. I am so small in front of thinkers of such magnitude immersed in legitimate thoughts, here I am finding hope for fair, ethical, sustainable governance that I can be inspired by and spread like seeds in the air, and that where they land, they sprout and become leafy trees, but I will stop philosophizing and focus on the good theories of when business is not just business.

In an orthodox environment, globally oriented towards governing for the purpose of generating capital, it is noticeable that people are concerned with developing ways to regulate and harmonize the relationship between corporations and individuals, such as the Triade - (United Nations Guiding Principles on Business and Human Rights) drawn up by John Ruggie in January 2013. Aware of the negative effects of globalization, listening to speeches expressing complaints about the unfavourable relations between companies and people, he spared no effort to strengthen human rights across the entire corporate spectrum. The struggle as described was arduous between countries, multinationals and human rights defenders, and what we still see today is a slow step towards integrating this will into government reality. This difficulty, according to the author, was due to the fact that it was something new, with diverse political interests. In order to overcome this difficulty, the strategy chosen was to create a special mandate to inform an existing list of the main business practices, reminding them of the role of the state, society and the individual. The hardest part was coming up with an idea on paper, in words, which was less difficult to get accepted; the challenge came later, when the mission became the implementation, the materialization of the norms. When we read this, we think that it was easy to institutionalize these three beautiful principles, but it took a lot of study, travel, cases and writing.

So what purpose do the guiding principles serve? I understand that it is to guide relations between corporate governance and individuals. But what for? As Ruggie says, to stipulate the detailed form of the steps needed for governments and companies to implement three fundamental pillars for business to live harmoniously with people, which are: Protect, where the state must guarantee rights and repress abuses committed, the second is Respect, a responsibility more directed at organizations, where they must avoid violating human rights, and avoid negative impacts and the third principle is Remedy, the need for greater access for victims to reparation for their wrongs, which can be through processes, responsible bodies and or judicial and extrajudicial actions. It's a nice equation to see: the state protects, companies respect and individuals can have access to remedies for possible harm. But as everything is not flowers, the triad is still beautiful to read and see. The power of multinational companies has expanded, giving them more power, more resources, so power and human rights usually run counter to each other, so concern has rightly arisen within human rights councils, a crisis has arisen in the world between having and being. Ruggie says, "Creating a company that is fairer in relation to human rights requires finding ways to make respect for rights happen in business, in other words, making it a standard business practice." Power and money are a difficult relationship to control in the light of human rights.

Traditionally in the world, economics has determined the right to have power, and those who hold more money respectively have more power. However, contrary to this, human rights were born to protect individuals from threats made by the state, which has the duty to protect. It is the state's duty to guarantee the rights of individuals and to protect them from actions that are inconsistent with the market. This issue is high on the international business agenda, and it's impossible to talk about business without emphasizing the importance of the people involved. The system of free trade, globalization and the opening up of the market all contributed to an escalation of business, without control and with an increase in the enslavement of people and social inequality. This same wave gave companies the right to operate globally, greatly increasing the rules for protecting foreign investors and intellectual property, a counterpoint in history, while the protection of multinationals for their capital increased, people and the environment were left without the same protection. Soon this inverse relationship of increased protection for corporations and reduced protection for people and the environment caused a chain reaction, with reports in 2010 claiming that a wave of suicides by workers were motivated by working conditions and abuses in the workplace. The greatest outrage is knowing that many pro-human rights activists in the companies indirectly contributed to such disregard when they bought the products legally. Business has always been and still is seen as a world that only exists to work for one side, that of money. If I'm getting richer every day, it's a sign that business is doing well, and actually, looking at it from the egocentric side of things, it's true, but the world wasn't made for just one person to live in, but at least for two at the beginning of time, in the hope that it would have been populated little by little, something that didn't happen. What companies forget, or so I feel, is that the same resources used to meet the needs of a million individuals, plus animals, flora, fauna, etc. These are the same resources that meet the needs of approximately 7.6 billion people, a figure from October 2017 available on the UN website.

Rights are for everyone and from everyone, companies, people, governments, nature. There is no magic formula for balancing the chaos between business and human rights. What does exist is the need to make routine and standard what is good for everyone, to do business not only within the philosophy of who wins the most and loses the most, but if we think of an ancient concept that is worth remembering, barter, let's do business in an exchange relationship, I need something that the corporation has, and in turn the company wants something that is mine, be it money, credit, goods among other ways of paying. What's important is that everyone assumes their role in this relationship. It's not about philanthropy, it's not about giving to those who don't have, it's about providing a business environment where everyone has the right to be independent and where their skills and competences can be recognized fairly. Encouraging, motivating, leading and teaching are superpowers that each individual can develop in their lives voluntarily and with a clear purpose: to be better people and thus build better businesses. Believing that changing habits is a first step can be a good path to success. You already have the guide, now you have to follow it. Remembering that we can't live without the intervention of the State is a fact, fortunately or unfortunately it is the one that manipulates the rules. Believing and contributing to the fact that corporations will respect every relationship that exists between them and people is another big step forward. No one, not even a ferocious animal, should be trapped without the prospect of rescue. The way forward is with: commitment, studies, research, monitoring by regulatory bodies and always being ready to start again if things don't go according to plan.

Postmodern ethics.

So much so that we write, talk, debate, dialog and philosophize about the blessed and eternal ethics. Be it modern, post-modern, ancient, old, traditional or even innovative. It doesn't matter what terms and times it's used in, what we see is its use at the pleasure of those who want it for their own ends. Ethics is ethics, a set of actions that must at least think of others. The world's problems, wherever they may be, are still problems, new or not, and they need to be solved, preferably from the perspective of ethics. So to better understand Bauman's work, let's look at what modernity is and what post-modernity is. First of all, the author distinguishes between modern and post-modern attitudes and ethics and places them outside the scope of moral concepts. Baruman pushes our thoughts towards understanding basic questions about ethics, such as: Is it possible to have ethics without morals or morals without ethics? Have times evolved and have ethics kept up, or do people simply care less about ethical and moral issues? These are complex conclusions to reach. In a social context where the exploration of the consequences of this criticism of post-modern ethics arising from attitudes considered modern at the time has caused a great deal of mental confusion, modern or not ethics is being good, being good is not doing bad to others. It is humanly impossible to believe that we are essentially good beings, that is, ethical, in a society washed in the blood of innocents by the actions of man.

As the author says, we are essentially good human beings, but we are also essentially bad. Both statements are correct, we are in fact the fruit of the initial human relationship in our lives. People are not perfect, so the world is not. Modernity has brought individuality to people, thus generating the need for economic and personal autonomy. As a result, the logic of things that until then would have been natural to human beings ceased to be so logical and decisions had to be taken differently. The world was evolving, the global process of things was already a reality, and what had previously seemed very obvious was no longer so. Modern society ushered in a new post-modern society, born out of the industrial revolution, with the advent of globalization interfering in customs, values, beliefs and standards, establishing a new way of looking at ethics. Leading people to treat morality as something that needed to be planned, determining what is moral and what is not. Morality is understood as a set of rules, standards and norms acquired in a society through culture, education, eating beef in Brazil is moral, while in India this attitude is considered amoral, it hurts the customs of that region, so eating beef in India is unethical because I am hurting the values and customs of that people. This reinforces the ethical dilemma: the moral crisis in the world has repercussions in the form of an ethical crisis.

Controversies in the study of ethics and morality are present all the time. Baunan says that "freedom means the right to model oneself", in other words, if I am what I am, I can say that I am ethical and moral, but it is worth remembering that not all men are endowed with morals and ethics, so we will not have a homogeneous society in terms of ethics. And self-love, which determines my actions, guides me towards my pleasures and strives to prevent me from feeling any kind of pain, and in order to achieve this, it is necessary to provoke decisions that go against ethics and morals. Man doesn't do evil to others out of real interest, but because he is seeking his greater good, his pleasure, his satisfaction, he doesn't morally remember the moral judgment, the one who believes in his own salvation, his well-being, or even doing good for the sake of good. Finally, this two-way street between morality and ethics brings a dilemma beyond man's comprehension. On the one hand, the freedom to make the decisions one deems necessary, and on the other, the need to limit one's freedom of choice for the sake of others. Post-modernity has brought with it the need for human beings to be more intelligent, to have more wisdom and knowledge. This body of knowledge will enable them to make better choices, and for dilemmas to be something temporal and fleeting.

Every evolution brings with it positive and negative points, and so it is with post-modernity: while it has made the world more flexible in terms of thinking and understanding, it has also generated a "re-enchantment" of the world with people, even though there are still so many unethical and moral struggles and wars. The relationship between reward and punishment in society further underpinned the relationship between the practice of ethics as something determined and not innate, that was born with the individual. But what are the moral limits of ethics, how do we identify them and how do we proceed? These are key questions for living in a community in a society that increasingly lacks clear standards. Every day, the paths lead us more and more to the "I" and the collective "we" - only if we could glue all the "I's" together, as Bauman says. Anti-dualist societies are what we had to live with. So why insist on the universality of moral norms in a mutual way if moral subjects are immoral in certain ways. In the construction of the "we", what can be seen is the strengthening of the "I" empire. Bauman puts it this way: "I always have a greater responsibility than everyone else". From a moral perspective, yes. The moral, ethical subject generally suffers from the loneliness generated by the gaze of the self, unable to see the world around them and interact with it without placing themselves above good and evil. You can't idealize a universal ethic for everyone and everything. People should realize that having morals and ethics doesn't necessarily need a reason or foundation.

What we feel is the freedom of choice and the lack of standards for these choices has created an ethical crisis in the world. We live in a society where almost anything can be done, and if you think about it, everything is justified, and the most barbaric and cruel atrocities of man can still be appealed against and defended. What kind of ethics and morality is this? Are human rights for humans? Are laws for the good or the bad? Honestly, the end must be the opportunity for the beginning, because even silence has its share of responsibility in this web of signs and meanings. Bauman says that the saints are those who don't hide behind the broad shoulders of the law, many of which are designed to defend the wrong. The salvation of post-modernity lies in seeing the self in the we that surrounds us. It is through traditional, modern and ancient ethics that we must make post-modernity the existence of the multiplying self. A conflicting relationship between proximity and responsibility: the closer we are to something, the more responsibility we have, and it is this relationship that frightens those who want to practice ethics: the more I know and practice, the more responsible I find myself.

The ethical universe is a living system that suffers from external interference. It's a nervous system, where we are, we suffer, we conflict, we generate solutions all within the rules of the game established by society. I believe in the state of being ethical and not being ethical, the path is the morality of processes, standards, customs and beliefs. Postmodern ethics, suggests Marc-Alain Ouaknin, "is an ethics of affection". The hand that caresses remains characteristically open, never closing into a claw, never grasping to hold" it exchanges without squeezing, it moves in accordance with the shape of the body being caressed. In simplest terms, it's by giving that you receive and only give what the other person should really receive. For every evil there is a remedy, so there is also a cure for relationships in the world, and strategies must be thought out and studied. The mission of civilizing the world and its relationships cannot be left to the responsibility of ethics and morality. The world is no longer "I", "we" and now "we are" is the word.

There is no first and second, there is a third, which is society as a whole. Priority now means "being first", not "best". The ancients quote that it is more promising to give more news of ruin than of prosperity, in order to prepare people for the difficulties of life, and to take on a role of preventing evil. This action is called the ethics of prevention and not the utopian ethics of progress and perfection. Believing in the best while preparing for the worst is the end of the beginning of any civilization.

Is ethics possible in a world of consumers?

To talk about consumption and ethics, we need to reflect on people's habits. What was once right may not be today, what was once ethical is now questioned. To understand the relationship between ethics and consumerism is to understand the evolution of human desires and needs. Maslow, a psychologist and scholar of human behavior, said that the basic needs were five - physiological (the basic need to eat, sleep), the second need to feel safe, then the social need linked to the need for status and esteem, which occurs after the social needs have been met, and finally the need for self-fulfillment, which are at the top of the hierarchical pyramid: morality, creativity, spontaneity, self-development and prestige. Understanding the world associated with ethics and consumption in the face of human relations is a challenging task, at the very least a battle between the contexts of reason and emotion, obstacles, planning or not planning, guiding questions for this dialogue. We live in a society where many truths are unquestionable simply because no one has ever questioned their obvious truth. For this reason, it is accepted as truth and serves as a starting point for deductions and inferences of other truths depending on the theory. Questioning an individual's relationship is therefore a matter of scientific theoretical construction, without ties or axioms.

We can't let the threats of fixed concepts, biased towards one reality, become an absolute truth, everything must be questioned and become an opportunity for new studies and understanding of the human relationship, so I raise the question - does Maslow's pyramid need updating? Are we going to let the feeling of axiom dominate reason? As Bauman says, life moves fast and it's difficult to keep up with the comings and goings, so trying to anticipate some facts and plan can be a viable option, but it's no guarantee of success. Human beings essentially try to find a cure for everything, so reconciling freedom and security in this constant variation of life is easy, and so it generates a feeling of insecurity and fear. The world tends to become a more complex place in which to live. Customs, values, respect are fragmented among us, we depend on each other for our present and future, is what the author says, and sadly I agree, we are independent beings totally dependent on each other. And to further problematize relationships, patience is a visit that must be almost omnipresent at all times, people don't talk face to face, technologies win out and put themselves between one another, not as a link, but as a constant threat between them. These increasingly indissoluble and complex threats provoke hurt feelings, emotional discharge at the maximum level of unbearable discontent among people, because everyone always puts their individual interests above the collective. The "I" is king in relationships and this is the great challenge of ethical life in a society corrupted by the ease and permissiveness that globalization has brought to the world.

The incredible thing is that according to Bauman, "globalization means that we are all dependent on each other" how? If we are more and more ME. But the explanation comes at a gallop, as the ancients used to say: if we are individualists in a world where we should be collectives, helping each other, it means that "the hell of the living is not something that is yet to come: if there is one, it is the one that is already here, the hell in which we live every day, the one we form by living together." So, by the way, that's the explanation, because the account of human relations in the world doesn't work, they want to divide what was made to add up. Man once feared the uncertainties of nature and its storms, floods and droughts, now it is man's own actions that are feared. One of the conditions for something to be called civilized was for it to be governed by human beings, called rational beings, and everything that escaped this concept was eliminated from the process of civilization, the objective was to eliminate ignorance and uncertainty, I see that we are still struggling to achieve this objective, because the uncertain and ignorant world we live in is notorious. There are so many wars for no reason, endless threats to the lives of others, ignorance in its purest translation reigns throughout the globe, actions such as the holocaust, genocide, the cold war, prejudice are still alive, hot and latent in the lives of the people, it was not in past centuries, it is here in this future planned one day to be different from what we have. So what is left for us in this individualistic, consumerist and capitalist society? As the wise say, we can talk, we can cry, we can even philosophize, but we must never stop fighting for better conditions for all peoples, that is living.

We have memories, and we need to use them to improve the world. Those who have lived through the horror of war, who have too much suffering inside them, must shout out to the world what they have lived through, but the shout is to inhibit new wars, it is to show through their pain how cruel a world at war is. We have choices for the same life experience, I can use it to improve the world or to make it worse, I decide which way I go, if we live ethically we will choose the best, the shared life for all. Bauman puts it this way: "Give power to the truth, but without humiliating them. Instead of acting on your impetus, don't insist on becoming this sterile soil, letting it overflow from your angry sacred lips..." Let's be witnesses to a reality, whether it's good or bad, but let's be sowers of good fruit and good news to those who are waiting for us. We live in unbridled competition and where there is only competition there will always be losers. The key question is not whether we are competing, but what I am willing to do to win. This is where the danger of humanity's collapse lies.

The challenge is to play a game with few rules but many collective challenges. I won't win if I do it just for myself, but I won't find many who want to play together and win together and share together. The world has become too tolerant to the point where this tolerance is bad for those who live in it. "The world is no longer docile enough to knead and mold; instead, it seems to overshadow us," says Bauman. I like Hegel's idea: "Intellectuals have begun to exchange their fantasies of conquering eternity for those of building a better future." I would venture to say that the idea of the eternal man who would remain for seed is an outdated thesis, now the law is to think that the future is near and the wise are preparing for it. The watchword is freedom and with it threats and opportunities, freedom of expression, freedom from oppression, spiritual freedom, ethical and moral freedom, but this freedom is imprisoning man in it, making him a freed slave. A choice? No. A consequence of insane attitudes that have no basis in life or in the environment. However, it is necessary to have "positive" freedom, as the author preaches, the freedom that gives us the right to come and go, the freedom to associate with our fellow citizens, the freedom of collective autonomy. We know that social problems have always existed, aggression, bad language and they continue to exist. But we need to fight against bad habits, customs. According to Michel, an individual can create their own identity, they don't need to follow existing ones, especially if they are bad for society. Bauman says that the life of consumption is a life of rapid learning and forgetting.

When we learn to consume, we also learn to forget the reasons not to consume. A real boycott of the ethics of consumption. How many times do you ask yourself if you really need something before you buy it? And how many times have you consumed and then realized that you could have lived without it? So these are the questions that should guide consumer society. Promoting unnecessary consumption is the role of this type of system, while social systems should promote awareness of positive consumption. We live in a society of instant and disposable consumer needs. The issue is individualistic consumption, which is determined by a pace that is only increasing every day, while it is in collective life that we suffer the consequences. Ethical value has lost out to aesthetic value, the collective to individualism, reason to capitalization and being to having. And so the days go by, and the future belongs to God alone.

Life for consumption.

The purpose of life in society has changed over the course of human evolution and the interference of consumerism in their lives. The question is whether people live to consume or consume to live in order to provide. In a society of appearances and insecurity, consumption is an option for self-affirmation. Every purchase is followed by a photo that will be posted on social networks to achieve a record number of likes. Bauman says that objects have taken over the world, and it's true, the imperative feeling is that we live for others, and personal fulfillment depends much more on the approval of these people than on the state of happiness we may feel. The problem with these habits is that they expose a lot of personal information, and the feeling of happiness that the system promotes is a threat to the life of each individual who is part of these systems. Bauman says that "users are happy to reveal intimate details of their personal lives." Social problems are inevitable, community life is necessary, but with rules, limits and freedom. A wide-ranging life, multitasking, different people, different cultures, different desires and needs, all connected in a large network.

Professionals need to look holistically, using analysis, observation and respect to ensure success in life. "Companies need to identify the least valuable customers" is the order of the day, but is this ethical? Maybe not, but it's profitable, and life is now about consumption. Human beings are becoming less rational and more cyborg-like, with organic parts but programmed intelligence. Companies are building a database capable of selecting potential consumers for their company and discarding all others, which is frankly yet another way of segregating people from the general context of living in a community. The three cases reported in the press in England show the evidence of this segregation, each case commented on by Bauman, as he says that social networks are a wave, and that these users like to show themselves too much according to him, but he does not fail to assume that social life is something inevitable and for young people not to be exposed on social networks is a social death. The second case, as we mentioned above, is a segregation of people, which is already done with social classes, from A to F, ranking these users, and detailing that they can lie about their data. And the third case is a system whereby only immigrants with the profile defined by them are attracted to the country, with only the most intelligent people within the established standards being able to enter the country.

What can be understood from these three cases is simple: people don't consume products, they are the product itself. We live in a consumer society and, just like things, people have to have reasons to be desired, and we are always on the shelf and not in the depository of life. In management, we could use marketing to promote ourselves on these channels, and what we're expected to do is get to know less and less about the real essence of people. Bauman believes that a network is not essential for life, but rather a community, where you get to know those who live in it. In a community, it is much more complex to disconnect from people, while on a social network it is simple and without major consequences. Life for consumption is a consequence of the lack of relationships between people. Romanticism for Bauman is the concept of liquid love, which says that nothing is solid, everything is marked by the insecurity of life, by the ease of disconnecting. Consumer culture directly interferes with the way people relate to each other, and Bauman in his utmost wisdom treats this relationship ethically and respectfully,

The author reveals: "The producer society, the main societal model of the 'solid' phase of modernity, was basically oriented towards security." How can we live for security in a world where uncertainty is the greatest certainty? And when there is no plausible and possible solution, people behave irrationally, seeking to base themselves on patterns, routines of individual behavior. 'But the human desire for security and the dreams of a defined "stable state" do not fit into a consumer society. This desire for stability becomes a danger, where people consume more and produce less in a sustainable way. Everything revolves around the internal war between what I need versus what I want. There was a time when conceptualizing need from desire was simple. As Bauman says, "A concept was once more solid, but now everything is more liquid." Nothing is certain and can be questioned at any time. If a concept is to be built, it must be born ready to die without too many struggles. Uncertainties create many gaps for debate and restlessness.

The central idea of this work is that the search for ideal happiness is non-existent in the eyes of human beings. So, to try to achieve it, individuals are doing almost anything, with the vast majority believing that happiness is on a shelf in a store anywhere in the world, promoting a tidal wave of consumption. "The possibility of populating the world with more affectionate people and inducing people to be more affectionate does not appear in the panoramas painted by the consumerist utopia, it is a dream that may become real," if it does, it would be a great step towards a happier future for everyone. If we talk about consumer culture, the peculiar way of saying that people are making choices that are different from what they should be, the consumer society represents the type of society that promotes, encourages and reinforces the choice of a consumerist lifestyle and existential strategy, rejecting all alternative cultural options to consumption, says Bauman. Consuming shouldn't be a bad thing, we are beings with natural needs, so we will always need to consume, the problem is the lack of control of this consumerism, the feeling is that if we don't consume the air is missing, hunger increases, something goes wrong, it shouldn't be like this. People in less or no favorable financial situations strive to be part of this consumerist nation that has transformed the world.

Bauman says that the main objective of consumption in a consumer society is not to satisfy needs, desires and wants, but to fulfill the idea in people's minds of consuming. We no longer buy what we need or want, the situation goes beyond that. Today, we consume on impulse, for social reasons and also for status, all of which leads us to think that happiness is there and will be the target of other people's consumption. This concept goes beyond the common sense of consuming goods and services, it promotes the collective thought that people are also negotiable products, in other words, merchandise at the world consumer fair, just like faith, ethics, family, values and other "things", everything has become merchandise to be negotiated. Nations negotiate the right to rule, families auction off their loved ones, spirituality has become a mega-business, even a little corner of heaven can be bought.

We were created to live in groups, together, collaborating with each other, whether in a community as idealized decades ago or in a network, connected online. The important thing is respect for differences, freedom of choice, the preservation of nature and relationships. We cannot accept society becoming "liquid", empty of values, fragile in its existence. Consumption is not the bad medicine for building an active, liberated and independent society, the mistake is the dose applied by people. Consumer culture has reached unbearable levels in terms of both relationships and natural resources. Bauman says that the life of the consumer, the life of consumption, doesn't refer to acquisition and possession, it refers to making movement in the community, the balance of this movement is what needs to be adjusted. People can't be commodities, there must be a real need or desire to buy, we can't consume for the sake of consuming. Evolution cannot lead to a decline in the political and social development of the world. As Bauman says in liquid modernity, I am what I buy, everything is change, nothing is constant, everything causes fear. Consumerism is where people feel they can find the certainty, the ground they lack, and the meaning of life that completes them.

Prosperity without growth: a good life on a finite planet.

So what is finite? It's what has a firm, a limit, like planet earth, which was created to house flora and fauna in balance with two Guests Adao and Eve, to enjoy all its resources, which were finite billions of years ago, so talking about prosperity is talking about the result of the actions of interaction between people and nature. Obama (2008) said in a speech: "I think all of us here today recognize that we have lost our sense of shared prosperity." In other words, we are an individualistic society that doesn't care about each other. What we see is the building of a prosperity without a future without positive growth, the lack of balance is evident between countries, nations, peoples and even residents of the same neighborhood and city. According to Jackson, we survive "in a world of finite resources, constrained by strict environmental limits, yet characterized by islands of prosperity within oceans of poverty." The increase in revenue from actions that are not suited to collective needs only tends to worsen social and economic inequality and increase the challenges of living under a capitalist and consumerist economic system.

People, companies and governments need to admit that there are limits to everything, including the growth of the planet. Concern about limits is very old, according to reports, dating back to when the world itself was created. Like what happened at the beginning of everything, (for those who believe in this line), there in heaven when everything was allowed, everything could be consumed, there was only one limit, one item, a single fruit, from a single tree existing on the entire planet could not be harvested for consumption, it was the danger of sin, the limit to the prosperity of the planet, but what happened? Man chooses to ignore the warning and breaks the limit of what is acceptable, between not consuming and guaranteeing prosperous growth, the Collective is left behind, he chooses to satisfy his desire and eat the forbidden fruit, and the consequences of this choice are felt from generation to generation. Limits were made to be overcome, but with the proper respect and knowledge of the consequences.

We are beings made to evolve, but this evolution must go hand in hand with an increase in the quality of life of people and the planet, but what we see is that this is not happening. Every day, people face more social and financial problems: the rich get richer and the poor become miserable, unable to maintain even their physiological needs, taking nature with them. The economic system becomes a casino, a game of win-lose, where poverty is gaining in numbers while the rich become an elite class of the chosen. The growth of cities contributes to the inequality of growth, situations such as health, food, education are not being made available as they should be.

In the business environment, companies need to be part of this movement to promote prosperity and growth, guaranteeing the continuity of life on the planet. Jackson suggests several paths that can make a profit and still help people prosper. One of these paths is for companies to offer more services than products. Focusing on the provision of services requires manpower, i.e. jobs, income, more people working and the system moving. Another point is that profit should not be the center of attention, or the only objective, companies need to innovate their processes for the benefit of the collective and not just the safe, it is difficult for a corporation to think like this, everyone undertakes for a single reason, money, but thinking that resources are finite and if they are not preserved now the company will be left without producing in the future, it can be said then that producing with sustainability is guaranteeing money in the future for the organization. Everyone has blamed globalization for the glories of the 20th century,

however, it is people who make decisions and not a wave, a system or a decade. There is no point in looking for culprits for this reality, there is not one, but a set of villains, society, governments, companies, consumerism, capitalism, etc. What happened was that nations went into debt in search of prosperity in order to grow, they didn't make plans, they didn't look at the whole picture, they didn't see the consequences, so a redefined vision of prosperity became necessary.

Sardar says: "Prosperity can only be conceived on the condition that it includes obligations and responsibility towards others." As long as people are individualists, full prosperity won't happen. Meeting the material needs of the collective is one way of understanding prosperity. Remembering that quantity is not the same thing as quality, serving the collective is much more complex. The struggle is to make society understand that mass production is not something prosperous and will not guarantee growth for the planet, nor will it guarantee a quality of life for people. For example, if I have R$8,000 to distribute in technology to communities that don't have access to it, I can use the concept of prosperous growth and buy enough smartphones for more than 20 people, or I can use the principle of desire and not necessity to buy just one smartphone from a recognized brand and give it to just one person. Jackson would say that measuring in these circumstances is even more difficult, as they interact with questions of psychological satisfaction. So to grow or not to grow? To mass produce or to produce for the masses?

Baumol's words "people in rich countries don't realize how good things really are" are based on the popular saying that only those who have experienced pain know what it's like. The theory goes that prosperity is not based solely on income, but on quality of life, but of course it is understood that there is no prosperity without economic growth, what we are trying to defend in this work is the exercise of balance between growth and prosperity. So many countries are already suffering from growth without real control, without effective prosperity, that they can serve as examples and motivators for a change in attitude. As Jackson says, as long as there is a thousandth of a second, there is a chance to change the outcome of the game. The formulas to guarantee this change are varied, from the arithmetic of growth to the one that shows the results between the relative and absolute mismatch ratio to the one that talks about the impact of three factors: population size, income and technology to bring about prosperity and growth. Efficient management of all these resources is necessary in order to meet the advances in demand, giving priority to the preservation of the social and ecological system, since none of these is yet capable of adequately serving the world's 7.6 billion people.

The equation for the heroic attempt to collaborate with this prosperous growth is to go slow, to slow down life. As The Economist says, "as any hunted animal knows, it's not how fast you run that counts, but whether you're slower than the rest." It's a survival strategy, they say the hasty eat raw, and it's true. Rushing with the consumption of life is hastening the arrival of a future that is not yet ready to receive all of us. The former suffered from a lack of resources. Society is swallowed up by anxiety, which in some cases turns into fear, says Jackson. It is known that fear is not all bad, it is a guide, but anxiety corrupts, generates insecurity, and insecure people tend not to make good choices. Companies do need to get the economy back to growth. The author suggests some practices, encouraging unemployment to produce lower wages, reducing interest rates and putting more money in people's pockets by cutting taxes or increasing benefits. But honestly, of all the author's ideas, the one I feel most strongly about is job creation.

In order to create a world with a better quality of life, prosperity and growth, we must be able to unite the economy with ecology, the individual with the collective, act today with the future in mind. Time is getting short, but there is still time for a greener and more solidary life,

BIBLIOGRAPHICAL REFERENCES

Aktouf, Omar **Post-globalization, administration and economic rationality: the ostrich syndrome** / Omar Aktouf; translated by Maria Helena C. V. Trylinski; technical review Roverto Costa Fachin. - Sao Paulo: Atlas 2004.

Alvater, E. **The end of capitalism as we know it**. Rio de Janeiro - RJ. Civilizaçao Brasileira, 2010.

BAUMAM, Z. **Life for consumption**. Rio de Janeiro: Zahar, 2008

BAUMAM, Z. **Life for consumption**. Rio de Janeiro: Zahar, 2008JACKSON, T. **Prosperity without growth: the good life on a finite planet**. Sao Paulo: Planeta Sustentavel. 2013

BAUMAN, Z. **Is ethics possible in a world of consumers?** Rio de Janeiro: Zahar. 2011.

BAUMAN, Z. Ètica **pós-moderna**. Sao Paulo: Paulus, 1997.

BECK, ULRICH. **Risk society: towards another modernity**. Sao Paulo: Editora 34, 2010.

Clegg, Stewart, R.; Hardy, Cynthia Hardy; Nord, Walter R. **Handbook of**

Organizational Studies: reflections and new directions. Volume 1. Sao Paulo. Atlas, 2001.

Giddens, Anthony (Org.) **The global debate on the Third Way**. Sao Paulo - SP: Editora UNESP, 2007

HART, S.L. **Capitalism at the Crossroads**. Porto Alegre: Bookman, 2006

JACKSON, T. **Prosperity without growth: the good life on a finite planet.**

Sao Paulo: Planeta Sustentavel. 2013

RUGGIE, J. G. **When business isn't just business**. Sao Paulo: Planeta Sustentavel, 2014.

SENNET, R. **The corrosion of character: personal consequences of work in the**

new capitalism. Rio de Janeiro. Record, 2008.

SENNET, R. **The Culture of the New Capitalism**. Rio de Janeiro: Record, 2012.

Solomon, Robert C. **Ethics and excellence: cooperation and integrity in business** / Roberto C.

Solomon; translated by Maria Luiza X. de A. Borges, - Rio de Janeiro: Civilizaçao Brasileira, 2006.

More
Books!

Printed by Books on Demand GmbH, Norderstedt / Germany